FIVE STEPS TO LIVING CHRISTIAN UNITY

About the
5 Steps Series

The books in the 5 Steps Series are useful for anyone seeking bridge-building solutions to current issues. The 5 Steps series presents positive approaches for engaging with the problems that open up gaps and divisions in family, school, church, and society. Each volume presents five short chapters (or "steps") on a single topic. Each chapter includes a relevant "excerpt" from a prominent writer, "insights" from the author, and an "example" to consider. The "example" is a real-life story that illustrates how each step can be applied in daily life.

FIVE STEPS TO LIVING CHRISTIAN UNITY

Insights and Examples

Callan Slipper

New City Press
of the Focolare
Hyde Park, New York

Published in the United States by New City Press
202 Comforter Blvd., Hyde Park, NY 12538
www.newcitypress.com
©2013 Callan Slipper

Cover design by Leandro de Leon
Book design by Steven Cordiviola

Cover photo is courtesy of Citta' Nuova Magazine, Aug. 2011 issue (081123966.jpg).

Experiences printed with permission from various issues of *Living City* magazine

Library of Congress Cataloging-in-Publication Data

Slipper, Callan.
  5 Steps to Living Christian Unity / Callan Slipper.
     pages cm
  ISBN 978-1-56548-501-3
  1. Church--Unity. 2. Ecumenical movement 3. Christian Union. 4. Church controversies. 5. Interpersonal relations--Religious aspects--Christianity. I. Title. II. Title: Five Steps to Living Christian Unity.
  BV601.5.S55 2013
  262.001'1--dc23

                              2013031462

Printed in the United States of America

Contents

Introduction 7

Step *1*

See the Need: Why Bother? 11
Excerpt: Chiara Lubich —
 "Mutual Love among Churches" .. 12
Example: *We go to Church as a Family* 17

Step *2*

Find the Way:
 Who Should Rebuild? 19
Excerpt: Cardinal Walter Kasper —
 "Healing the Wounds
  of Separation" 20
Example: *The Life We Shared
   Made Us One* 25

Step 3

Construct the Building Blocks:
  All the Little Things 31

Excerpt: Flora Winfield —
    "We Become the Church" 32

Example: *When Tragedy Strikes:
    The Amish Community and I* 36

Step 4

Listen to the Silent Third:
  Our Traveling Companion 39

Excerpt: Rowan Williams —
    "The Dimension of Unity" 40

Example: *May They All Be One* 45

Step 5

Overcome All Obstacles:
  The Strength of Weakness 49

Excerpt: Chiara Lubich — "I See Him" ... 50

Example: *Living for Christian Unity* 54

Notes 57

Further Reading 59

Introduction

*P*ROGRESS HAS BEEN REMARKABLE in the work for Christian unity. Much has changed since the Edinburgh World Missionary Conference in 1910 when it began in earnest, at first among Protestants. Indeed the tendency among some to feel a sense of failure is actually a mark of the opposite: so much has been achieved that it has become difficult to see what to do next. Most of the headline-grabbing and exciting things have been done: people pray together, attend one another's services, are gradually learning from one another and there is a sense of growing fellowship at all levels. But full unity, bringing Christians into a single, visible community, has not been reached and does not look as close as it did in the heady, ground-breaking days.

A key question that arises out of this new situation is one that has been and, in fact, is always valid. What kind of unity are we seeking?

It would be wrong to decry the work of doctrinal reconciliation, the attempt to set up co-operative, uniting or united structures, or the effort that goes into committees, reports, resolutions and all the (sometimes exhausting and dull) background work supporting the growth of Christian unity. But if unity is only about doctrine and organization it is, perhaps, in some ways almost a waste of time. It only goes a short distance in building God's reign. This is absolutely not to say that doctrine and organization are of no consequence. Indeed, they are essential to how full, visible unity can be lived out and demonstrated. But they are to serve unity, not be its substance.

The unity Jesus prayed for the night before he died was something immense. It was nothing less than the life of God shared among human beings. The Fourth Gospel shows Jesus praying: "The glory that you have given me I have given them, so that they may be one, as we are one, I in them and you in me, that they may become completely one" (Jn 17:22-23). Not only is this the kind of thing that would capture the attention of a troubled and weary world, responding to some of the deepest human longings, but it has the most amazing implications. It means that in Christian unity God, effectively and really, is present and active. Here and now God works upon, through and with those who are united. Unity makes God a direct actor in human history.

The struggle to reunite the divided church, therefore, is more than an add-on to the serious work of being a Christian. It is central to establishing the rule of God. For relationships of unity between people are where God is found. Worship, especially the sacraments (however they are theologized for the majority who have them), personal prayer in the heart's silence, the Bible all appear as doors onto God, doors wide open for God to come through and be with people. But they are all in places or times set aside specifically for this. Relationships of unity, on the other hand, are where God comes at any time and everywhere into the world. God is no longer separated, sometimes seemingly almost locked away. The Holy is not restricted to the sacred — either moments or places. Building genuine relationships of unity, within the churches and among the churches, is then both the end that must be sought and the very thing that must be done to achieve that end. Without this everything else is diminished, because a church where God dwells through genuine unity, in the variety of its peoples and expressions and understandings and ways of doing things, is a church where everything is touched with gold, the gold of the living, effective presence of God.

It is not easy. The five steps offered here, along with real-life stories from Christians of various churches that follow each step, are an attempt to explore and inspire something of this life of unity. They are presented as an organic whole, with the underlying logic linking them suggested in the title to each step, and they go from strengthening our motivation to seeing how, practically, unity can be lived. Each step also has a motto that attempts to encapsulate its meaning and may help in remembering it. All of them come out of real life, both my own and shared, since I write from within the experience of Chiara Lubich's spirituality of unity, which is both a personal discovery and a venture lived with other members of the Focolare Movement. What is put forward would hope to speak to anyone enquiring more deeply into their spiritual journey; it is most emphatically not intended only for ecumenical specialists — the enthusiasts for Christian unity who, in reality, deserve our thanks for their hard work in something so essential though not always acknowledged as such. Ecumenism, the search for Christian unity, indeed, only really makes sense if everyone is involved. It reaches out to all or it is not real unity. An ecumenism of the people, for all the people, therefore is unavoidable if what is sought is the Christian unity where God, truly, acts in and through Christ's Body on earth.

Step 1
See the Need: Why Bother?

Mutual Love among Churches

The only genuine Christian reconciler will be the one who knows how to love others with the very charity of God, which brings Christ to light in each person, which goes out to all (Jesus died for the whole human race), which always takes the initiative; that charity which makes us love each person as ourselves, which makes us one with our brothers and sisters, in suffering, in joy....

And the Churches too should love with this love.

"That the love with which you have loved me may be in them, and I in them" (Jn 17:26), Jesus prayed. And we instead are always ready to forget his testament, to scandalize the world with our divisions, a world we should be winning for him.

Over the centuries every Church, in some way, has turned rigid through waves of indifference and misunderstanding, if not of mutual hatred. What is needed in each Church is a supplement of love. Indeed, the Christian world needs to be overwhelmed by a torrent of love.

Love, therefore, mutual love among Christians, mutual love among Churches. That love which leads to putting everything in common, each a gift to the others, so that we can foresee the future Church with one truth, one truth alone, but expressed in different ways, seen from different perspectives, made beautiful by the variety of interpretations.

Chiara Lubich[1]

See the Need: Why Bother?

*M*Y BROTHER WAS DYING. The cancer was incurable, not to mention his other complaints. Fortunately he was not in great pain, and at that moment he had not yet been confined to his bed. I wanted to talk to him about God, not I hoped in a bossy, condemnatory or aggressive way, but simply to explore the possibilities of a greater life with the Infinite — a greater life that would touch him as his body's energy drained away and he journeyed into the dark, into the mystery. The time seemed right and so, hesitantly, explaining myself step by step, I broached the subject. After all, when we had last spoken about these things he was a churchgoer, a practice that by now he had almost totally given up.

He told me he had stopped going to church when, one day, he simply realized he did not believe any of it. He still thought that God must exist but that God was not much interested in creation, especially in him. As for Christianity, it amounted to little more than a pile of rather incredible myths. I knew what he meant. From his perspective it all looked like a hollow and hopeless form of whistling in the wind, with no basis in reality.

I said what I could. I reassured him of what I deeply feel: that it is not important so much that we believe in God but that God believes in us. God is love. I suggested some ways he could be open to this, though I doubt he took me up on them. The key thing, in the end, is God's mercy and I entrusted (and entrust) him to that.

But why did he not believe? He was an intelligent man, a man in many ways of his times, with the strengths and, perhaps I would have to say, the weaknesses of his culture. He was not closed to Christianity, but what the church offered said nothing to him. It did not seem to be true. I think in this he is representative of many thoughtful people.

The problem is not that Christians cannot express themselves, or put things in relevant ways, or offer meaning or comfort or inspiration. We can do all these things. Not always well, indeed sometimes rather badly, but at root, even when we manage to say it right, what we say, the meaning, comfort and inspiration we offer, seems to be a matter of dreams, at best a pretty poem, less substantial than the mist.

One reason for this dream-like quality seems to me to be fairly obvious. Our words are not backed up with facts. We are not so much describing things that we know about at first hand as trying to convince people of a set of ideas, a story. It does not surprise me that the parts of the Christian body where there is a sense of a living encounter with Jesus, a life touched by the power of the Spirit, are the ones that are growing the fastest. May they grow and prosper! These are people who can say what

God is doing in their lives, and what they talk about is an experience.

But just what is that experience? It is more, or at least it should be more, far more, than merely a feeling of personal salvation. If that is all it is, it can only convince a few. It may be about a feeling, a good feeling, intensely personal and liberating, but feelings do not necessarily make any comment upon reality. The critical observer, the intelligent person who tests out what you say against other experiences, will say that they are just about the way you see things, not necessarily the way things are.

What is needed is to see a total transformation, a whole new world, something that demonstrates by its facts that it is not just a feeling or a theory. This presents a challenge, also to the brain. If you see relationships renewed, a better way of working, a touch of real beauty, the laughter and happiness of people at peace in themselves and with one another, then it is hard to avoid the question as to whether what they think may not actually have some substance to it. Maybe, just maybe, they have a grip on something true. And if, amid this renewed world, you sense a presence that is not of this world, you sense Another who is the source and guarantee of the laughter, then you have to ask yourself if this is not an experience rooted in reality, a reality that is more real than that simply offered by your five senses.

This is the challenge offered by Christian unity. When Christians are united, then not only are they personally fulfilled, but the world they live in is transformed, with new, open, and deep relationships. These cannot stop at just the interpersonal but must touch upon and change the structures of everything: the way we use our money, the kinds of institutions we have, our laws and education, the art we produce, the way we do science, our psychological understanding and health care, even our buildings and the way we dress ...

The tragedy is that Christians are not united. We sit in our divided churches and hope that each of our groups can reach out to the world. It will never work, or at least never work well. Not only is our experience, for all its depth and reality, restricted, because we fail to taste what unity can bring, but, as it presents merely a half-realized picture of the new creation Jesus died that we might have, it does not speak to the questioning world.

Is it not time that we took Jesus at his word and put into practice the full implications of what he meant when, on the eve of dying for us, he prayed: "Father, may they all be one, as you are in me and I am in you, may they also be in us, so that the world may believe that you have sent me" (Jn 17:21)?

Real-Life Story
We go to Church as a Family[2]

I grew up in a small town in Pennsylvania. An important part of how I grew up is the fact that my mother and my siblings and I are Catholic and my father is Methodist.

My family goes to two churches every Sunday. We go to Mass at 8 a.m., come home, eat breakfast, and then go to the Methodist church service.

Our family's way of practicing our faith was explained to me very simply. I once asked my mother why we had to go to two church services every Sunday, and her reply still resonates with me. She said, "We go to both because we are a family, and we go to church as a family." For us, it is a profound way of showing love for each other. As an act of love for my dad, I go to church with him; as an act of love for us, he comes to Mass with us. This small sacrifice for each other is the kind of love on which my family is built.

Also I have to admit that I laugh when I hear my friends or acquaintances complain that church is "long" or they have trouble paying attention. I tell them, "You have NO idea!"

Because of this experience, I have grown up with a keen understanding of the differences but also the many similarities between Catholicism and other Christian churches. It has helped to give me a better knowledge and understanding of my own faith because of the questions and clarifications that arise from experiencing two different church services every week. When talking with friends from different churches or other Catholics, I find that I can understand and speak about the common heritage that we share with different Christian denominations.

In my family I have realized that while the differences between our churches are important, so is our love for each other. I remember my mother telling me how important it is to respect my father's belief even when I clearly disagreed with him. We have sometimes had discussions about these differences, but I have seen how much my parents love and respect each other and how my father respects my Catholic belief, and so I want to do the same for him.

Through our commitment to love one another, I began to realize how we are united in Christ because of our common baptism and that if we live mutual love He is among us (see Mt 18:20). My father once shared with me that meeting committed Catholics really encouraged him to be open to meeting and dialoguing with people of other churches and also people of different religions. I realize that, as a family, we would not be who we are without this influence. It's an aspect of my life that is truly a gift. When I encounter persons of other churches I see them as family, because that is the very concrete reality I have lived in my own family.

Step 2
Find the Way: Who Should Rebuild?

Healing the Wounds of Separation

First, Christians can witness to genuine unity in diversity by building a community that is peaceful within itself and that is not torn apart by internal polemics, ideological polarization or mutual recrimination. Wherever Christians live or work together, they can be encouraged to:

- Meet in their neighborhoods to deepen everyday relations of friendship, particularly among families;

- Foster relations of cooperation and shared commitment in the workplace and jointly address work-related or social issues;

- Express the values of their own traditions, keeping faithful to them without denigrating others or engaging in polemics;

- Avoid attitudes, gestures or actions that may hurt the feelings of Christians belonging to other traditions;

- Be generous and open in day-to-day relations with other Christians, trying to overcome inappropriate expressions of present divisions.

(continued)

Second, effective channels of communication and cooperation between parishes and local communities can be cultivated through regular contact between their respective pastoral ministers, together with those having responsibility for particular aspects of the local community's life and mission.

Together, local communities and their leaders can:

- Forward information to each other about major events and celebrations;

- Set up or support a local council of churches to enable their members to work together, engage in dialogue, overcome divisions and misunderstandings, engage in prayer and work for unity, and give, as far as possible, a common Christian witness and service;

- Facilitate and support ministerial associations or regular meetings between local pastoral ministers.

... This ecumenical cooperation is of vital importance, not only for greater effectiveness, but also for the sake of common witness and spiritual ecumenism.

Cardinal Walter Kasper[3]

Step 2

ONE OF THE THINGS I have learned is that it is usually good to say sorry. It has a very healing effect when there is a disagreement, even when I am not certain what it is I have done wrong. Of course, the challenge sometimes is to find the thing to say sorry about! At other times, less often, the wisest course is to stay silent. Any further discussion can make someone who feels bad, feel worse. It is not always possible to put the problem into words.

What we face in our personal relations is generally true for the relations between Christians and churches. Sometimes saying sorry is not enough or not the right response.

There seems to be no one-size-fits-all solution, no easy answer. Maybe there are some clear issues, questions of conscience where ideas clash, but there are legions of mere misunderstandings, misconceptions, and misinterpretations. These have been made worse by the divisions lasting so long. Our independent histories mean we have developed in different ways, and so the longer we stay apart the more there are prejudices, as well as new issues, to keep us apart. Then there are hidden issues too: antipathy to what is done in an unfamiliar or alien way, the vague sense that the other must somehow be trying to oppress me because in the past that group has oppressed my group, our distaste for things we do not understand and so seem somehow twisted or abnormal, the barely conscious feeling

Find the Way: Who Should Rebuild?

that my group must always be better than the other simply because it is my group. Trying to fit back together the bits of a shattered unity seems almost impossible.

But what if we reverse the terms? What if instead of starting from positions of division we start from being united? Why not take this radical relational leap and completely change the terms of the discussion? Would this not give us a different, rather less piecemeal, more effective approach? For we can cut through all the psychological hang-ups, be untouched by the clutter of false judgments and cease to be trapped by a remorseless logic of antagonism because of our contrasting convictions, if without superficiality we decide to accept one another just as we are and, accepting one another, deliberately choose to love one another.

That deliberate choice makes the difference. It brings about a completely new state of affairs. We no longer solve the problems in order to become united, we are united in order to solve the problems.

This is possible because our deliberate choice makes love for one another (and nothing else) the key to our relationship. It is this that unites us in fact and in reality, in our lives and actions, in our feelings and attitudes, here and now. The other things, the difficulties and questions to be faced, will not go away, but we will now face them differently.

When we come at things from the position of division, we come as various individuals or as various groups. The subjects who act are many. But when love for one another is the key to our relationships, the subject who acts is different: it is no longer many but, with all of us acting in harmony, it is both many and one. Individuals and groups do not disappear; indeed as a result of their harmony in love, they are enhanced, becoming more themselves. But at the same time they are more than just individuals and groups, because they live as one.

This, however, is not only an extension and an enrichment of the identity of each person or group of persons. Something else happens in our oneness. Open to the other, we become open to what is Wholly Other. This is a deep-seated openness to Transcendence. Indeed, as Jesus said, "Where two or three are gathered in my name, I am there among them" (Mt 18:20). In our mutual love, then, we are opened up not just to other human persons, but also to the One who dwells in the heart of every human person (see Jn 1:9). This One dwells among us and he acts.

He is then the One who gives us light to understand and sort out the complications. Instead of acting as scattered individuals or groups, we let him (in us, through us, with us) be the One to resolve the issues that divide us.

We so often short-change ourselves, when we could bring the enlightenment of the Infinite to bear upon our problems. Just think of the potential for theological discussion if Jesus were the One at work in the conversation. Why not let Jesus himself comment?

The One who should rebuild Christian unity, therefore, is not really us as individuals or even as groups, but it can be, should be, Christ himself. Our insights and questions, all that we have and are — even the points of contrast — are the raw material by which we can love one another, and never more so than when out of love, in order to understand one another better, we describe (with tact and detachment) points that are still matters of contention. And if our insights and questions are ways of loving, then they are ways that allow Jesus to be among us.

Made one by our love, we can allow the One to make us fully one.

Real-Life Story
The Life We Shared Made Us One[4]

I was born and raised in Boston. Seven years ago I went to live in a lay community in Fontem, a tiny village in the middle of a palm tree forest in West Cameroon. I spent six years there. The place is a Catholic mission including the Mary Health of

Africa General Hospital and its newly built infectious disease center, St. Clare's Parish Church, Our Lady Seat of Wisdom Boarding School (where I worked) and the St. Joseph the Worker School of Carpentry. Each is staffed by local professionals as well as some from abroad.

The interesting thing for me was that not all of us were Roman Catholics. There were Presbyterians, Lutherans and Baptists. This was somewhat of a novelty in the setting of a Catholic mission, although we all shared a deep Christian experience that grew out of a strong commitment to living the gospel. The gospel-based love that we tried to practice with each other and those around us was also striking because of the variety of Christian traditions that we represented.

In Fontem, I was joined by three others from El Salvador, Nigeria and the Philippines. There were also two local members in our community — a Presbyterian and Roman Catholic. Shortly afterward a Lutheran from Sweden joined us.

Living in a community with members from different churches was a new experience for me. Our life together was based on keeping the presence of Jesus among us through mutual love and living the gospel together (see Mt 18:20). Each month we would take a sentence from scripture, try to live it, and then share the results. Through our everyday experiences of living Jesus' words, I began to see that there truly was much more that united us than what divided us.

Whenever we sat down together for a meal, the table talk was similar for everyone. We would share how we had tried to see and love Jesus in the people we met on the dusty roads of the village, or in their homes, which were sometimes deep in the forest, or in our workplaces at the hospital or school. Everything was punctuated by our common effort to love Jesus. And each of us spoke of Jesus in the same way: there was no Catholic or Lutheran or Presbyterian Jesus in our house but only one, and he was quite alive among us.

Each weekend some of us went to visit the outlying villages, where we would share the life of the gospel with the local Bangwa people living in these remote areas. Together we worked in the village of Besali to raise money and build a small Catholic primary school and a Presbyterian church. The Catholics contributed new tin roofs for the local Presbyterian church and school when they were blown off during a storm. At their invitation, we attended all of their celebrations and they ours.

Peter, our Lutheran brother, was not able to attend services in his own church because the closest Lutheran church was located in Bafoussam, many hours away by public transport. But once or twice a month he would travel through the forest on treacherously muddy roads in order to reach a group of Lutheran Christians who gathered with their pastor for a weekly celebration of the Eucharist. We Catholics had no difficulty in attending Mass each day and receiving the Eucharist. Seeing Peter's effort made me see how I had often taken this great gift for granted and gave me a new appreciation of the opportunity offered me each day.

Since we seemed to share the Christian life in every other way, not being able to share the Eucharist seemed a sharp and painful contradiction. One day the local Catholic bishop mentioned that he could give permission for Peter to receive the Eucharist whenever there was no Lutheran celebration available. Peter wrote to his bishop in Sweden to ask his opinion, and the bishop, while hesitant at first, gave Peter permission, but also reminded him to obey his conscience.

Peter asked each of us what we thought. He shared that for him the life we lived together among us and with the local community was already the life of the church. We all nodded in agreement, understanding exactly what he meant.

But then Peter went on to say, "I think that we need to see this as a wound in the Body of Christ, which is still divided." Together we felt called to embrace and love Jesus in this suffering. So he continued traveling each month to Bafoussam.

At home we took every opportunity to pray together with Peter. In fact, other moments of prayer now acquired new and deeper meaning for us. Peter would always lead us at morning and evening prayer, sometimes using the Lutheran prayer book. While we were all at Mass, he would often stay home and read the Bible readings for the day from the Lutheran liturgy. When he would join us at Mass, we would offer the suffering we felt at not being able to receive the Eucharist together.

But it was a sorrow mixed with joy, because our desire for unity was already unity, and the life we shared with Jesus in our midst already made us one.

Step 3
Construct the Building Blocks: All the Little Things

We Become the Church

Working for unity will change us. It may not make us more like one another — it may give us a much more profound understanding of ourselves, but it will change us. Being in relationship always changes us, as individuals in our ordinary lives just as much as churches working together. We are transformed in our relationship with one another and in our relationship with God, and it is in this transformatory quality that our relationship bears fruit. We become God's agents for the transformation of human community into godly human community; we become the Church.

Which is why ecumenism is far too important to be left to ecumenists.

Flora Winfield[5]

Construct the Building Blocks: All the Little Things

IT IS PERHAPS A truism, but it is interesting nonetheless that tiny things, when they are banded together with other tiny things, are strong and can make a decisive difference: the saved coins mount into riches, the straw breaks the camel's back and the last snowflake cracks the branch. It is the principle behind democracy where every vote counts. It is why the union of the individually powerless can take on would-be exploitative employers or unjust rulers.

The same holds true for our apparently insignificant acts of love. They are crucial in bringing about a world at one with itself where harmony reigns, something most people yearn for but few seem to think actually possible. If it is ever to happen it will be built from the accumulation of good acts: so every single individual is challenged personally. There is no exception.

What I do in my own life counts.

My acts are an indispensable part of a love that goes and returns, a love that is shared, mutual. They are likewise indispensable in building up God's chosen (though perhaps not only) instrument for uniting the world: the church. If I, as a Christian, put love at the heart of my relationships with others from different Christian traditions, and they in return do the same to me, then together we make a living tissue of relationships, and at least one part of the Body of Christ comes alive. This, of course, can be done anywhere: on the street, at home, in the workplace, or in discussion groups, as well as in any activities specifically aimed at promoting Christian unity. If all individual Christians did the same, then the whole Body would become alive, and be active in the world. Christian unity does not depend upon the work of theologians or specialists or even of church leaders, although they too are involved. It depends almost entirely upon the love of individuals. If each one of us, however unimportant we feel we are (because we do not understand God's love that sees each child of God as infinite in value), loves like this, then unity — full, visible unity — is inevitable.

There is a consequence to this. It means that in the first place unity is in the hands of the people, all of the people, and in principle it must in some way include everyone, otherwise it will not be genuine or effective. After all, Jesus prayed that all may be one, not just those who were keen on unity (among whom would be included the sometimes undervalued "ecumaniacs"). Real Christian unity then is not simply a matter of agreement among remote authorities, but a fact that I live (or fail to live) with other members of Christ's Body.

And what an effect it has!

The greatest glory of any relationship of love I manage to build with my fellow Christians is that it allows Jesus himself to be among us. He is the One who draws together God's scattered children in his living Body.

Yet if I am to have the love that makes this possible, I have also to value the little acts, the daily attentions to others, the tasks completed with them in mind, the jobs done, the moments of listening, the smile or other gesture of consideration, all the myriad ways in which practically and with my muscles, I concretely act on behalf of the other person or persons. Such little things done by ordinary people, including me, are the substance of Christian unity.

To see this, of course, requires Wisdom. It is so easy to be dismissive of what seems, on its own, to be unimportant. Indeed, we tend to undervalue our acts of love and to do so can feel almost like a virtue, as if we are not giving too much value to ourselves. But even in the most inconsequential act of love badly executed, if there is the merest drop of real love, God who is love is present, and God is infinite. Each tiny act of love is thus limitless in value. We should expect more of God who is present than of our personal effectiveness or virtue which is absent.

With this real conversion to love that is God present in our acts, we can begin to act with greater courage, relying on God's grace at work in us. Nowhere is this more true than in rebuilding Christian unity. Every Christian doing everything out of love, including all the little things, brings it about.

It could seem almost too easy, were the kind of love involved not so deeply sacrificial. Its pattern is Jesus dying on the cross, the One who explains to us his personal command that we should "love one another as I have loved you" (Jn 15:12, see also 13:34). All that is required, then, is the genuine effort to make real, practical, down-to-earth, Christlike love the key to our relationships. When among us this is a fact, not a mere notion or vague aspiration, then Christ himself dwells among us. And when he is around, we should expect the unexpected.

Real-Life Story
When Tragedy Strikes: The Amish Community and I[6]

When I was a child, my sister and I used to stay at my grandparents' house while my parents took a vacation in an area of Pennsylvania called Lancaster. I remember how happy we were when Mom and Dad would return. They would tell us about their brief stay and usually would buy for us small but wonderful souvenirs. We loved the little dolls that they brought because they looked so different from the others we had: the boy doll was dressed all in black: pants and jacket, wearing a small straw hat with a round rim. The girl doll was dressed in a long black dress with a sort of bonnet on her head. We were fascinated by it all. My parents would then describe these special and beautiful "simple folk," as they are often called. Lancaster reflected their life style: religious people, God-loving people, whose farms reflected their love of God and nature.

As I grew up, my desire to visit this part of Pennsylvania grew stronger and stronger until finally one day I did, in fact, go there. I wasn't the least bit surprised at what I found. I was taken by the beauty of the Amish people, their lives, their lands and oh yes, their delicious food!

While there, I always longed to befriend an Amish family so I could share my life of love for the gospel with them, knowing that they, also, would share their beautiful life with me. And so it happened, through an Amish store-owner, that I was introduced to Emanuel and Katie Fisher. To meet them, eat at their home and share our values and life with them was as if I had met long-lost relatives. They were like family to me and I to them. Over the years our friendship grew ever more beautiful.

But then tragedy struck. On October 2, 2006, at the West Nickle Mines School in Lancaster County, Pennsylvania, a gunman took ten little girls hostage, shooting five to death. As soon as I heard the horrific news, I phoned the Fishers. Katie told me that one of the little girls killed was a relative of theirs. I immediately decided to go in order to be there in person to share the Fishers' pain. When I was there, Katie brought me to a garage which was the "temporary school" where the rest of the children were having class. The little school where the tragedy occurred had been taken down. In fact, all that remained was a fence with a sign: "No Trespassing." There were a few bales of hay placed on the area where a new school would be built.

Katie introduced me to Emma, the eighteen year old Amish teacher, who was credited with saving the lives of many of her students. It was a special moment, assuring her of, not only our prayers for her, but those of our entire community. As I met the other children who survived the tragedy, along with their parents, I was deeply moved as they repeated to me again and again: "Please extend our thank you to everyone who is praying for us. Ask everyone to continue to pray for us." I told them that we would, assuring them that we are all part of a large family and that we were united with them in prayer and love. We promised to stay in touch and we have ever since; that unbreakable bond of love and unity continues to this day.

Step 4
Listen to the Silent Third: Our Traveling Companion

The Dimension of Unity

Unity is first and foremost being in Christ through the Spirit. It is the unity of the very life of God; the unity in relationship of Father, Son and Spirit. It is unity with the mind of God, and with the works of God. In St. John's Gospel, chapter 6, we read of "doing the works of God." In the second letter of Peter we read of "participation in the divine nature" — the text which lies at the root of all Christian reflection on the subject of theosis, divinization. We read in the New Testament of praying the prayer of Christ, "Abba, Father" in the Spirit. Our Lord speaks again in the Fourth Gospel about drawing his disciples "to be where he is." St. Paul speaks of our "having the mind of Christ." They are the themes that run throughout the Farewell Discourses in St. John's Gospel, and which dominate for example the sixth chapter of Romans, the second and third chapters of 2 Corinthians and the first chapter of Ephesians. Those are only a few references among many.

That is the dimension of unity that is primary and that determines everything else we should say about unity: the unity that shapes everything else is unity in the work, and the prayer, and the mind of Christ through the gift of the Holy Spirit.

Rowan Williams[7]

Listen to the Silent Third: Our Traveling Companion

*O*NE OF THE THINGS that bedevils the search for Christian unity, or anything else that involves discussion, is the certainty of our own rightness. We are so sure the way we see things is correct and that others, in order to see things correctly, must see them as we do! What we tend not to notice is that, in the process, we have made ourselves the measure of truth. The truth is therefore what I think.

In reality such an assertion of personal conviction is a position of perfect integrity. And I cannot, with integrity, abandon my position.

Experience, however, teaches us something else, at least if we are attentive. Sometimes we are mistaken, sometimes others have a better understanding than we do, sometimes it is obvious that our understanding is only partial, our reasoning adrift, our information inexact.

Of course, humility would be a great help as it would allow us to see the truth we might otherwise be blind to, the truth beyond our immediate comprehension. But there is something even more important. In our discussions we tend not to see the nature of truth. We treat it as if it were only about intellectual propositions, a mere matter of ideas. Truth, however, is more than something we can capture with our thoughts or frame with our words.

It is worthwhile pausing for a moment to consider this more deeply. It may seem abstract, but it has real and decisive impact — in the search for Christian unity as in every other area of our lives. The answer to the question "what is truth if it is not just about ideas?" is something that may seem at first glance to be a shocking or strange assertion.

Truth is a person. It is Jesus who is the eternal expression of God in human form. He is the reality at the root of all reality. In him we see the real nature of things. And what we see reveals to us the pattern things must follow to be true to their real nature.

Finding truth, therefore, is encountering a person and so, if I copy this person in my life, I live the truth he is. Likewise, if I share his way of seeing things, I see them as they are.

Truth is therefore something outside of me, or better someone, to whom I must accommodate myself. Truth measures me, not I measure truth. Integrity in this case is not so much following what I think, but seeking to adapt my thoughts to him, to Jesus.

At the same time, he is not only outside of me. Since he is the reality of all things, he is the reality of me too, and in finding him I am finding my true self.

What is more, since he is God made human acting in history and so in the here and now, my relationship with him can be of a very particular kind. He can bring me to dwell within him, make me, as it were, him in him. Sharing in him, I share in truth and live it out.

The wonderful thing is that in our discussions, our talking together, I can meet this truth who is a person. This is the opportunity of having his presence among two or more met together in his name (Mt 18:20). As we open up to one another in love, so we open ourselves up together to him, and we come therefore to see things even more clearly, catching his vision. He, who is truth, opens the eyes of our understanding to what is true.

I remember once five of us were trying to choose some wallpaper. This may not seem much, trivial even, but it was a kind of question of truth. Looking at a catalogue filled with various options, the question we were asking was, in effect, what would truly look best and, given the current styles, be such that people visiting the house would feel at ease? The truth we were seeking was what would be most fitting at that moment and we hoped to perceive it with Jesus present among us. Everyone had a different idea, some widely contrasting, and there was a modicum of tension. But bit by bit, as we sifted through the catalogue, offering our ideas without trying to force them on one another, like a light dawning upon us, we came to a decision we all shared. It included in some way all the points that had been put forward, even the ones that had been discarded. With Jesus the truth to show us, we saw what none of us had perceived on our own. Needless to say, we all liked the result!

Now, the same can be done with even more contentious issues.

But, whatever the issue, this living process is as demanding as it is rewarding. Certainly we have to be able to think: what we are doing is reasoning together, and so the capacity for logical clarity should be honed. We need also to be sensitive to our intuition, and so the capacity to recognize truth with our gut has to be finely tuned. The immense talents of reason and intuition are thus gifts we use to love one another. And it is this love that brings us into truth's real, personal presence. It is a love that means being free of everything, capable therefore of losing everything, even our ways of understanding, for the other. Thus the truth as we see it individually becomes a tool for seeing truth more fully. When things are unclear we do not need to think more, but to love more.

This is, it has to be said, a deeper integrity than simply affirming my personal conviction. It means readiness to discover something new that, while it contains the thoughts that have led to its being perceived, also transcends them.

For that to happen, obviously perhaps, two things are needed: one, to recognize that together with the others I am on a journey to *a fuller grasp of the truth* already dwelling in me and, two, *the ability to be detached* from what

I think, offering it as a gift and waiting for the arrival of a new, deeper understanding.

Among us, if we love one another, there is a silent Third; it is Jesus who, despite his physical quietness, is eloquent — just as he was on the Emmaus road (Lk 24:13-35). Together we should listen to him as he speaks in the inner chambers of our hearts. He is waiting to re-explain his teaching to us. If we let him, not only will we find ourselves united, but ancient wisdom will speak with modern clarity.

Real-Life Story
May They All Be One[8]

I was born into a Christian home in which my parents deeply loved God, the Scriptures, and the church we faithfully attended several times a week. I cannot recall a time when I did *not* care about the things of God. Aside from a brief period of wrestling with doubts in college, I have loved God and desired to know him my entire life….

Then, in 1995, everything changed for me. As I was saying the Apostles' Creed during a Sunday morning worship service I experienced my … conversion. The Holy Spirit took my heart to the "Lord's Prayer" recorded in the Gospel of John:

My prayer is not for them alone. I pray also for those who will believe in me through their message, that all of them may be one, Father, just as you are in me and I am in you. May they also be in us so that the world may believe that you have sent me. I have given them the glory that you gave me, that they may be one as we are one — I in them and you in me — so that they may be brought to complete unity. Then the world will know that you sent me and have loved them even as you have loved me.

(Jn 17:20-23)

... As I soaked my soul in the prayer of Jesus (John 17), my vision for the unity of the church increased. My love for the church became more than a concept; instead, it developed into a deep, growing love for the church as God's people.

As I unpacked the insights the Holy Spirit was giving to me, I sensed two things. First, I realized I couldn't love what I didn't know. I knew very little about the *whole* Christian church, even though I had a good grasp of church history. I knew there were three different historic Christian churches — Catholic, Protestant, and Orthodox. But I knew very little about what these three great churches believed and why. I knew something about the intra-Protestant differences via disagreements and schisms. But I knew much less about the core truths shared by all Christians everywhere. I soon discovered what is called classical Christianity. I read materials from various churches, traditions, and theologians. I tried to read what churches had written about themselves rather than what others had written against them. What my reading and listening uncovered was nothing short of amazing. It became clear that there was much to learn from the wider body of the Christian church.

Second, I knew that I couldn't be satisfied with loving a *concept* of the church. So I set out to find God's people, to get to know people outside of my own tradition. At first, this seemed like a daunting task, but I began by taking one small step at a time. I made it a personal priority to meet with Christians who were different from me. Before long, I was relating to an ever-widening circle of new friends....

Today, my passion for the church has led me to monasteries and Methodists, to Anglicans and the Assemblies of God, and to a growing respect for Mennonites and Moravians. It took me, an evangelical and a Reformed Protestant, deeper into the words of Luther and Calvin, who left a profound mark on a large portion of the Christian church. To my great surprise, it propelled me back to the church fathers and the Christian past — a past that is both Roman Catholic and Orthodox....

One day as I was reflecting on these things, I realized that the idea of the church that I had embraced for well over forty years was just too small. God had taken me on a journey and had deepened my love for this church in ways I could have never expected or imagined.

Step 5
Overcome All Obstacles: The Strength of Weakness

I See Him

What is the best way to overcome every personal or collective disunity?

In both cases, I must say this: "If he has taken upon himself every suffering, every division and trauma, I can think that wherever I see a suffering, I also see him. This suffering reminds me of him; it's a presence of his, a face of his."

And like him, we too must not stop in the cracks of division. If Jesus re-abandoned himself to the Father who was abandoning him, in like manner we must go beyond and overcome the trial, saying: "In this suffering, I love you, Jesus forsaken, I want you, I embrace you!"

And if we are so willing, generous and attentive to continue loving what God wants from us in the following moment, we experience that, more often than not, the suffering disappears, as if by a divine alchemy. It's because love calls forth the gifts of the Spirit: joy, light, peace, and the risen Lord in us takes the place of the forsaken one.

And what fruits come from loving Jesus forsaken whom we recognize in the lack of full communion among our Churches?

There are very many. First of all, the union among Churches that it has been possible to achieve so far is a strong witness to the Gospel, in which the painful fact of the not perfect and visible communion and its consequences are faced with constructive courage and peace.

Chiara Lubich[9]

Overcome All Obstacles: The Strength of Weakness

THE SIGN OF THE cross has been much abused; nonetheless it is true that "in this sign" Christians conquer. The cross is the emblem of Christians because it is the source of the new life they experience. It is common to all the followers of Christ, and so it is also a place where all Christians meet. It is where Christians are one.

And just as the cross, in reality, was an instrument of shame, a brutal form of torture that displayed in graphic terms how the crucified was despised as a fool (for the Greeks), cut off from the political community (for the Romans) and utterly rejected by God (for the Jews), so we too meet under its shadow with a certain sense of shame. It is not simply that before so great a sacrifice by the Innocent One who was God made human, we have nothing to say. The worst thing is that we continue to negate his gift. He died forsaken by earth and heaven to unite earth and heaven and all of us with one another: the most profound oneness. And we are divided.

Yet because of his gift this very same negation can be the source of its opposite. In his becoming nothing, the forsaken Jesus transformed nothingness. He took all that was not God, all that was contrary to love which is God's nature, and filled it with himself, filled it with love, with God's nature. He became nothing out of love; so love invaded the negative.

This is why the cross is the sign of our triumph. But it is more than just a sign. It is also the means of his triumph in each of us personally and among us in our relationships. It is a past event that continually transforms the present — if we let it.

If I, as an individual, accept whatever pain and darkness I go through, embracing it fully, letting the agony happen, then I find not the agony but the One who fills it. I find Jesus. This is his triumph in me.

But for the triumph to be effective, this letting myself be fused into one with the agony must be so total that, after my initial yes to it, I am free to look beyond it. It is as if I hug something so tightly that it becomes me and my arms are then free. I can then pick up whatever I have to do next as an act of love, following God's will. This is the moment of a sudden dawn. I discover the life, joy, light, love that Jesus is and enter the splendor of the resurrection. Here I find new energy to be for others. My way of being, however frail and with whatever uncertainties and failures, has become the same as his: Jesus' way of being for others.

Doing so, I open up in divine love to others. If they do the same, they open up to me in the same divine love. That love then unites us. We are one in God, entering the resurrection together. This is his triumph in us: relationships in God.

If a group of Christians, united in this way, open themselves up to another group of Christians, or if a church opens itself up in this way to another church, what they find will also be relationships in God. And in this real, living, present, unity they will find God alive among them.

This is the main way of overcoming all of the hurts that, contrary to the gospel and often contrary to plain common sense, Christians have inflicted upon one another. It is the way of making fuel from our failure, our continuous frailty a source of strength. It is the way of having Truth dwell among us so that we are led together to a greater understanding of Truth, going beyond the partial perceptions (partial however true they may be) that each of us has. It is the way of not denying the bad and the painful but of journeying into it (into Christ crucified in it) and so going beyond it.

In the end, this is the most practical (and the most efficient) platform from which to bring about Christian unity. All of the other work, the theological conversations, the symbolic gestures of acceptance, the declarations of intent, the setting up of structures by which we can act together, the praying together and the making of friendships, is certainly vital. But more than all this is the spiritual ecumenism of the cross.

The cross, or better the One dying on the cross, our shared emblem, is our shared means for reaching the goal.

Real-Life Story
Living for Christian Unity[10]

My commitment to living the gospel, and in particular its call to Christian unity (see Jn 17:21), helped me to go back to my Antiochian Orthodox Church, to learn more about its riches and be faithful to all its teachings. I also became more active in my parish, by helping in the church school. My husband also belongs to my church. Together we choose a sentence from the gospel each month, and often share how we live it throughout the day. It helps focus our day and put God first in our decisions and actions.

It is true that many times I, as well as my family, feel the pain of the division among the different churches. I feel this especially when I am with my non-Orthodox friends at their church and I cannot receive the Eucharist. However, I have learned to recognize Jesus crucified and forsaken as the key to unity. In him are contained all the sufferings of humanity. So each time I feel this suffering, I unite my small pain to his and offer it to the Father for the unity that Jesus prayed for.

Real-Life Story

My commitment to working for unity in the church led me to attend two weekend meetings of members from different churches, which took place in Rome. It was a strong experience to meet members of many churches, from the Anglicans, to Lutherans, Reformed, Orthodox, Coptic, Assyrian and so on. At first, we had to face the walls that separate us, the differences that set our churches apart, and that we cannot change. We did not have any easy resolution to certain moral and ethical questions that we face in our daily lives. There were difficult moments of deep suffering. On the other hand, we all had a commitment to increasing unity, so we searched deeper for what unites us. Of course we went back to Jesus, his Word, which is the same for all churches. Putting into practice the Word, we each listened to the other with greater charity. We learned about the different churches, trying to see unity through their eyes. We prayed together and attended each other's services at different churches. We realized that we each have many riches, and that we can make room for each other by living mutual love with radicalism. At the end of the meetings we had no resolution to some pressing questions; however, our mutual love was stronger, and we were enriched by this strong experience. I felt that we were able to stop the walls that separate us from growing higher.

Notes

1. Chiara Lubich, *Essential Writings: Spirituality Dialogue Culture* (Hyde Park, NY: New City Press, 2007), p. 326.
2. As shared by C. S. (who asked to remain anonymous).
3. Cardinal Walter Kasper, *Handbook of Spiritual Ecumenism* (Hyde Park, NY: New City Press, 2007), pp. 73-75, 76.
4. As shared by Bill Hartnett.
5. Flora Winfield, *Growing Together* (London: SPCK, 2002), p. 129.
6. As shared by Gail C. Giacobbe.
7. Rowan Williams, Address at 50th anniversary of Pontifical Council for Christian Unity, 17 November 2010. (See http://rowanwilliams.archbishopofcanterbury.org/articles.php/803/archbishops-address-at-50th-anniversary-of-pcpcu.)
8. As shared by John H. Armstrong in John H. Armstrong, *Your Church is too Small* (Grand Rapids, MI: Zondervan, 2010), pp. 27, 29, 30, 33.
9. Chiara Lubich, *Living Dialogue* (Hyde Park, NY: New City Press, 2009), p. 57.
10. As shared by Aline Farkouh.

New City Press
of the Focolare
Hyde Park, New York

New City Press is one of more than 20 publishing houses sponsored by the Focolare, a movement founded by Chiara Lubich to help bring about the realization of Jesus' prayer: "That all may be one" (John 17:21). In view of that goal, New City Press publishes books and resources that enrich the lives of people and help all to strive toward the unity of the entire human family. We are a member of the Association of Catholic Publishers.

Further Reading
All titles are available from New City Press.
www.NewCityPress.com

Gospel in Action	978-1-56548-486-3	$11.95
Building Bridges	978-1-56548-203-6	$12.95
A New Way	978-1-56548-236-4	$12.95
Living Dialogue	978-1-56548-326-2	$9.95
Our Age	978-1-56548-081-0	$9.95
Walking Together	978-1-56548-526-6	$19.00

Scan to join our mailing list for discounts and promotions

Periodicals
Living City Magazine, www.livingcitymagazine.org